Little things

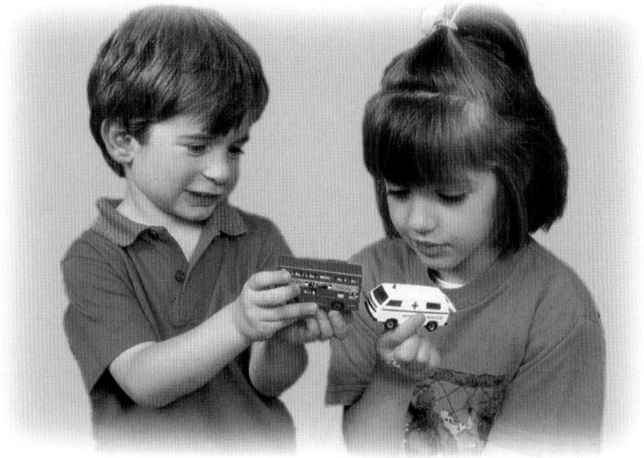

My truck is little.

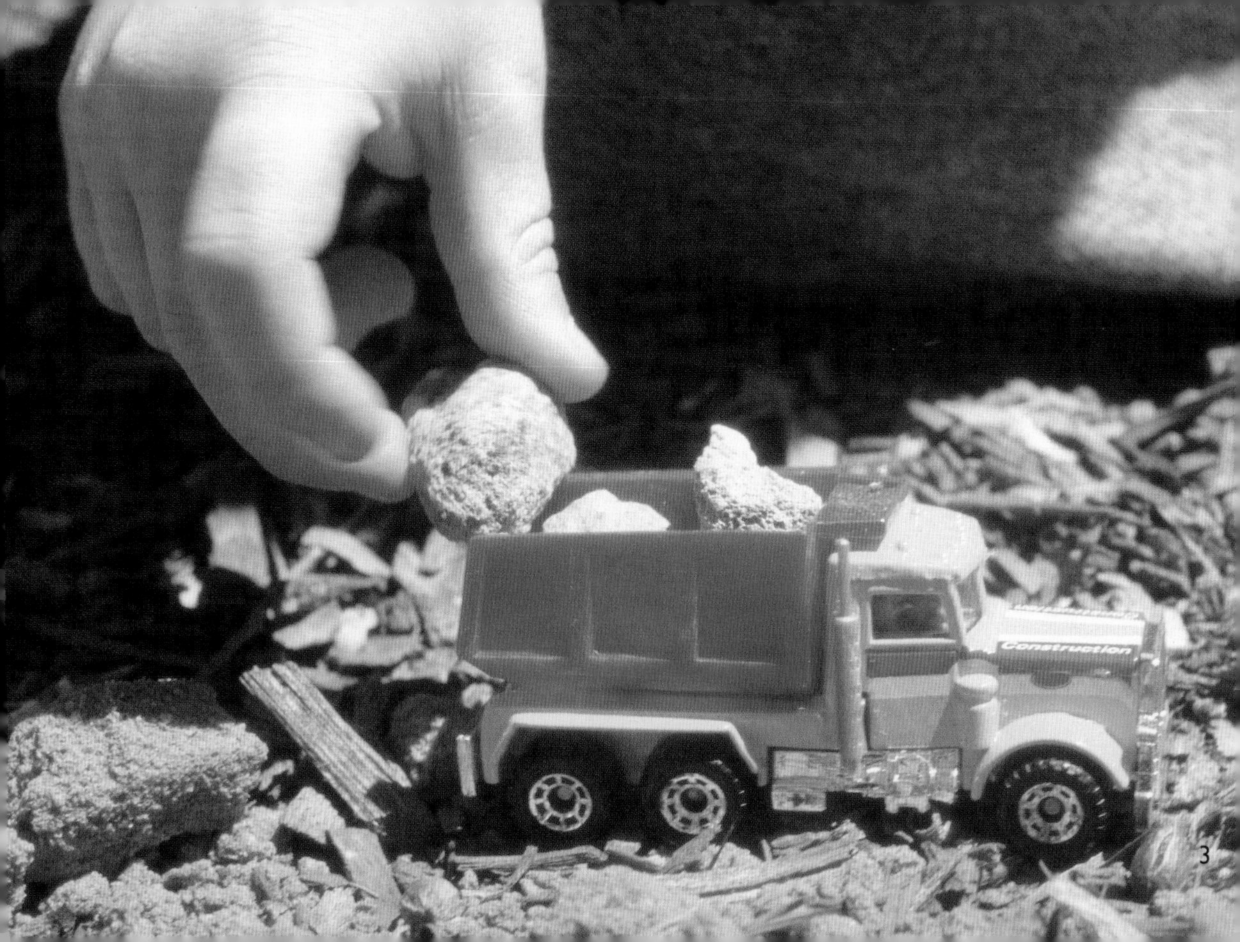
Construction

My bulldozer is little.

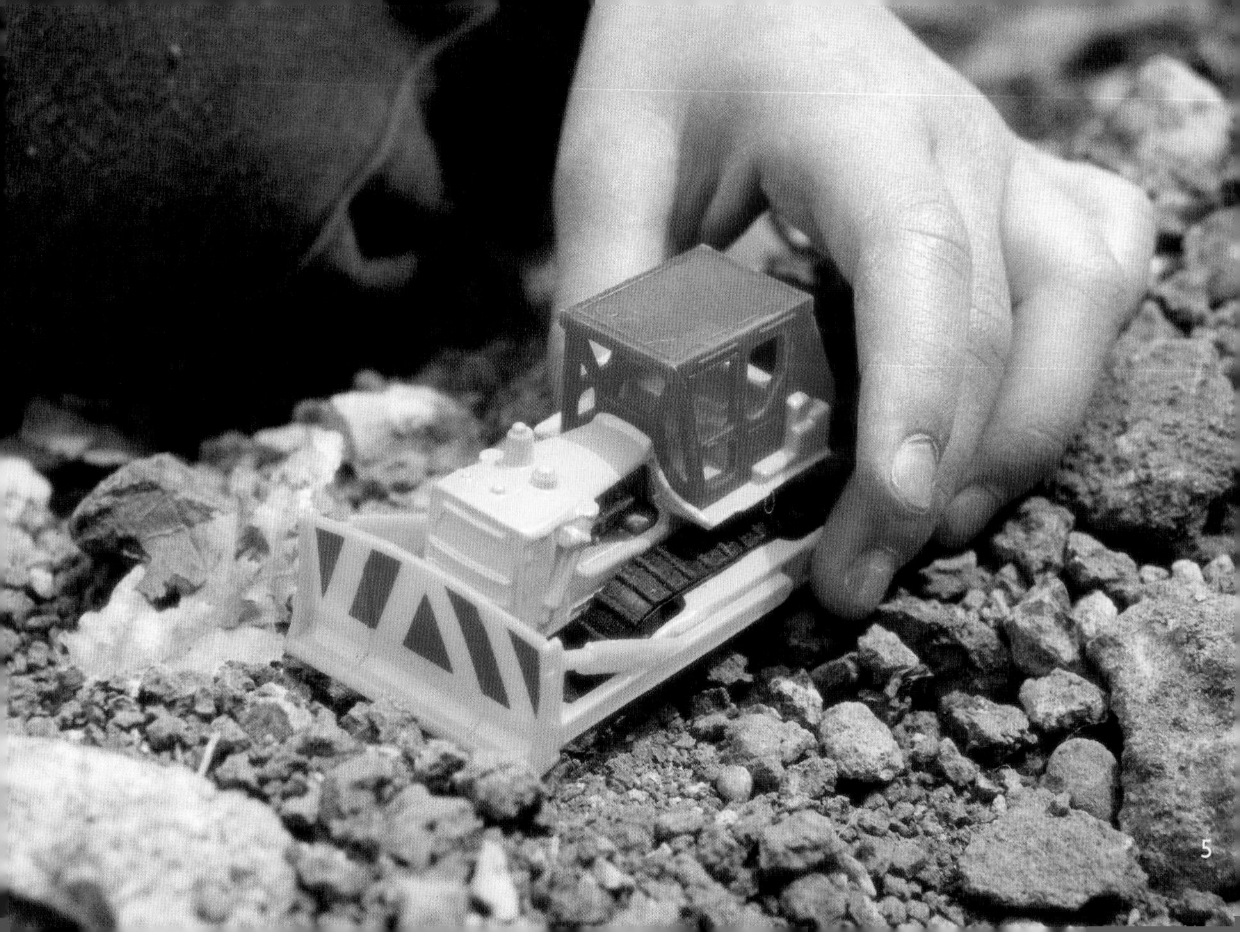

My ambulance is little.

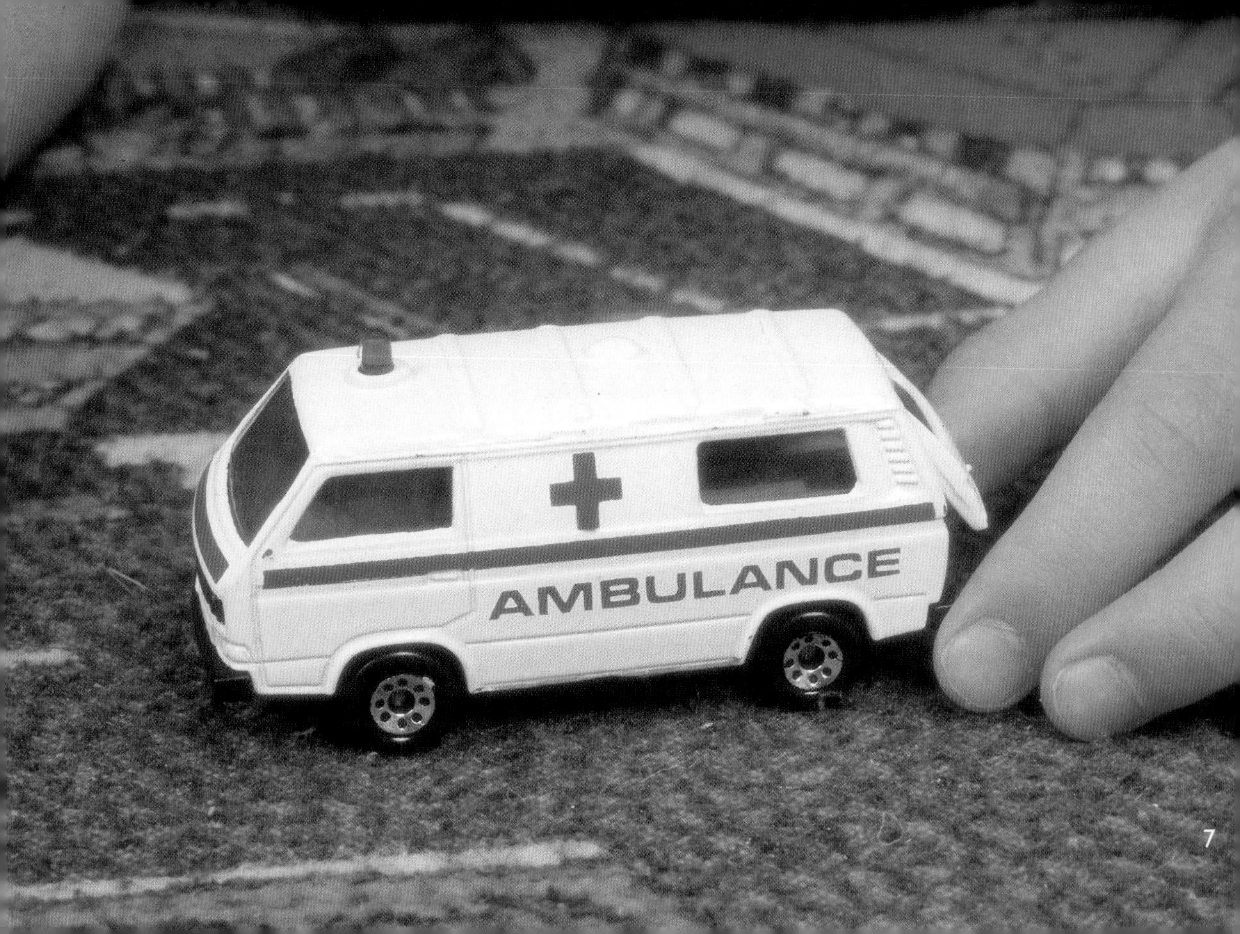
AMBULANCE

My fire engine is little.

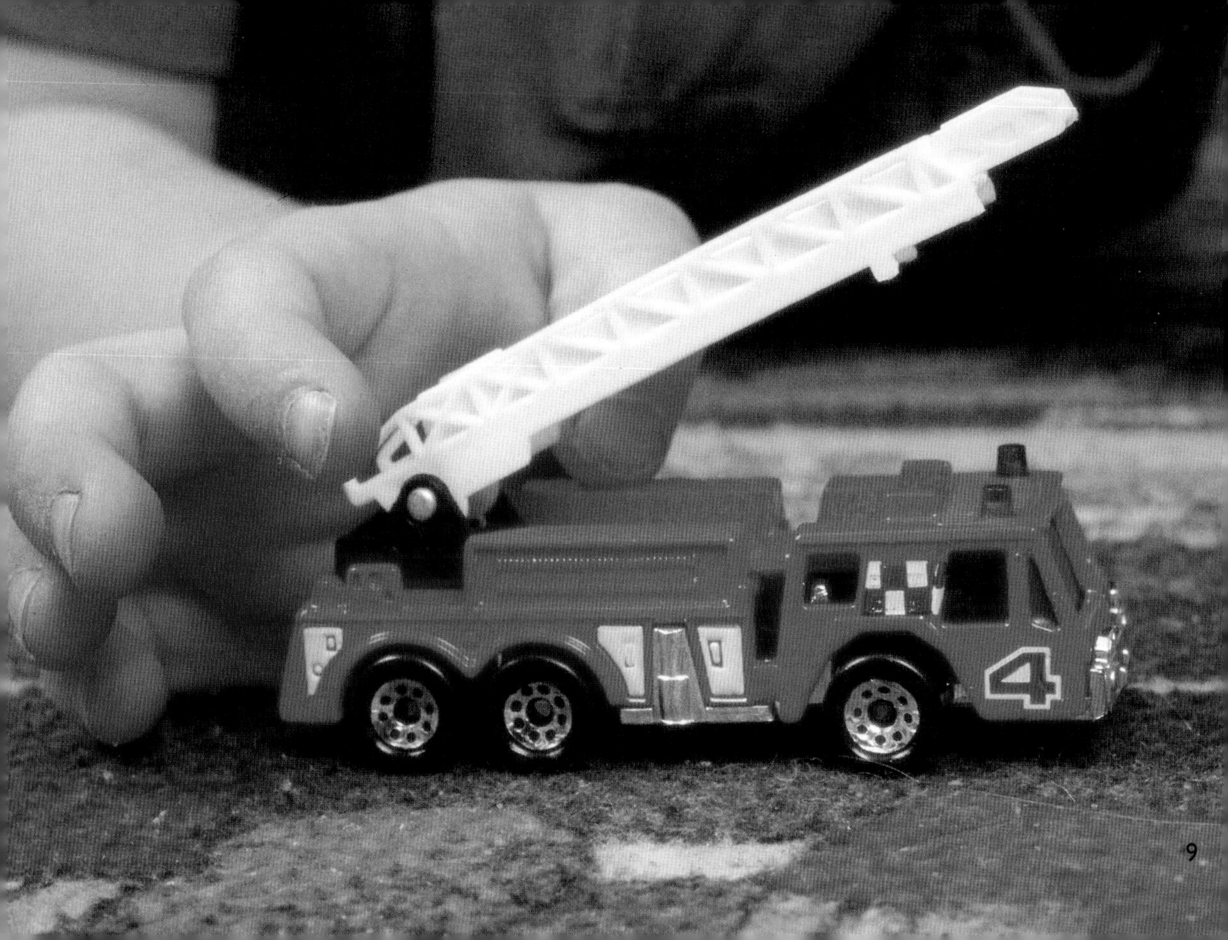
4

My bus is little.

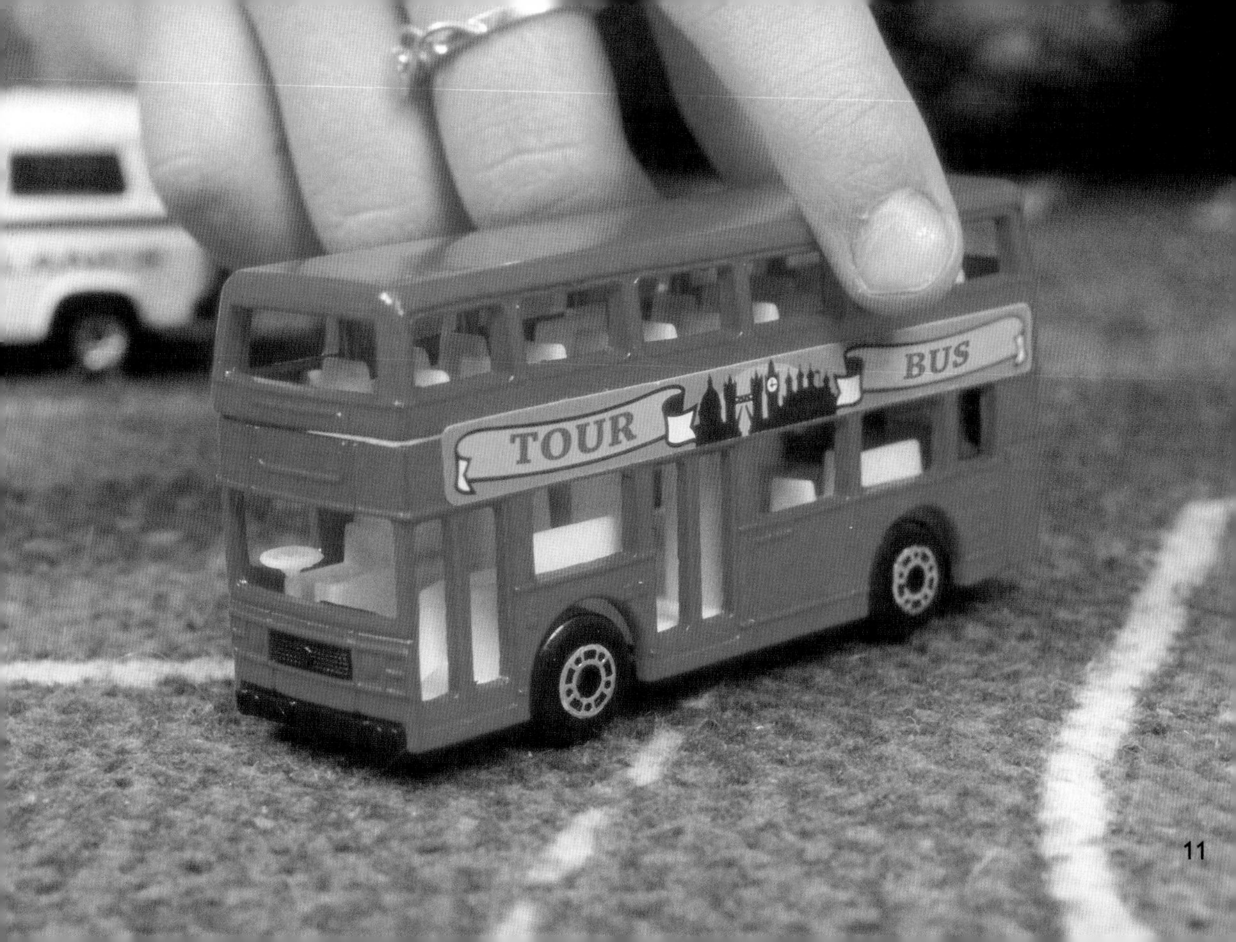
TOUR
BUS

My crane is little.

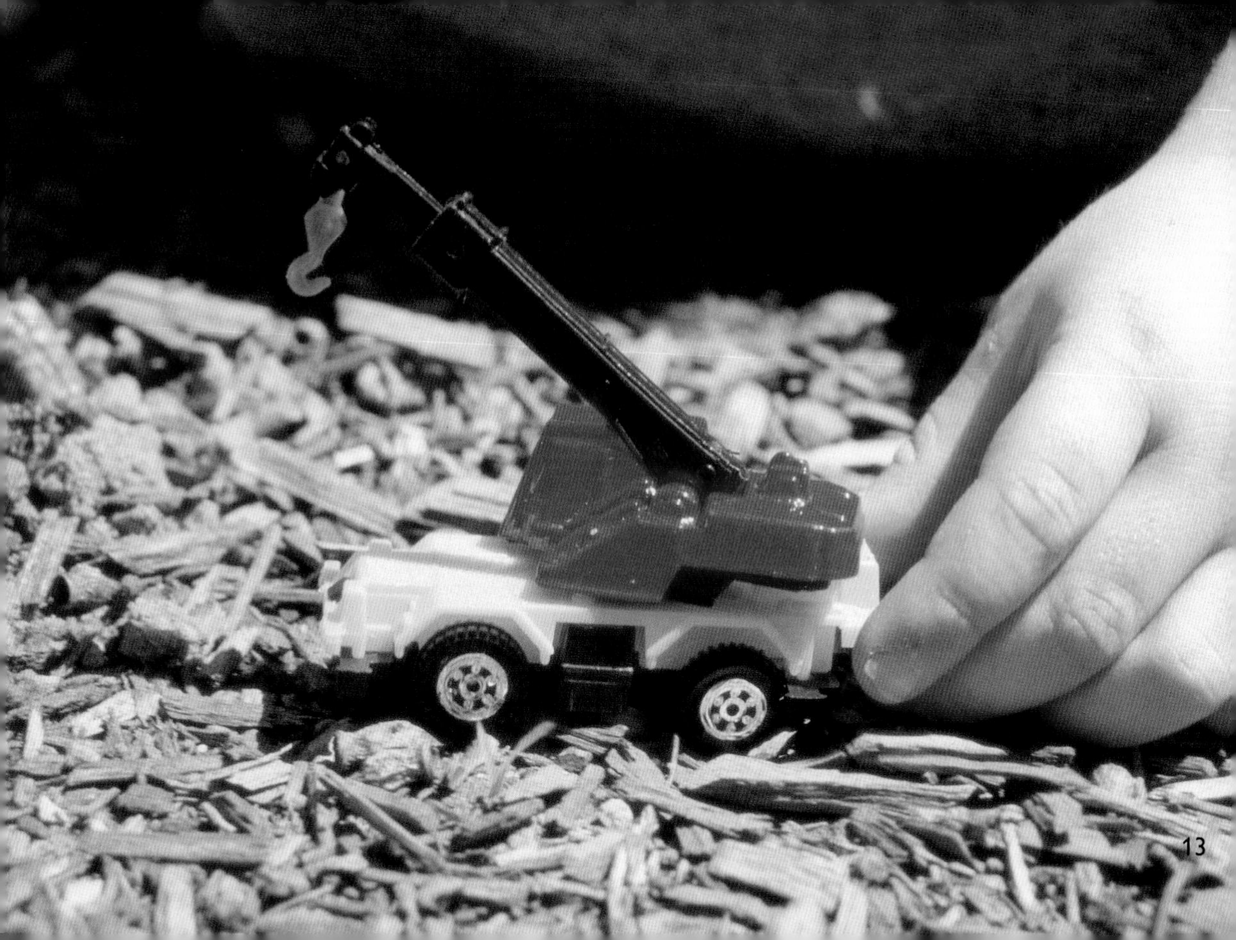

My plane is little.

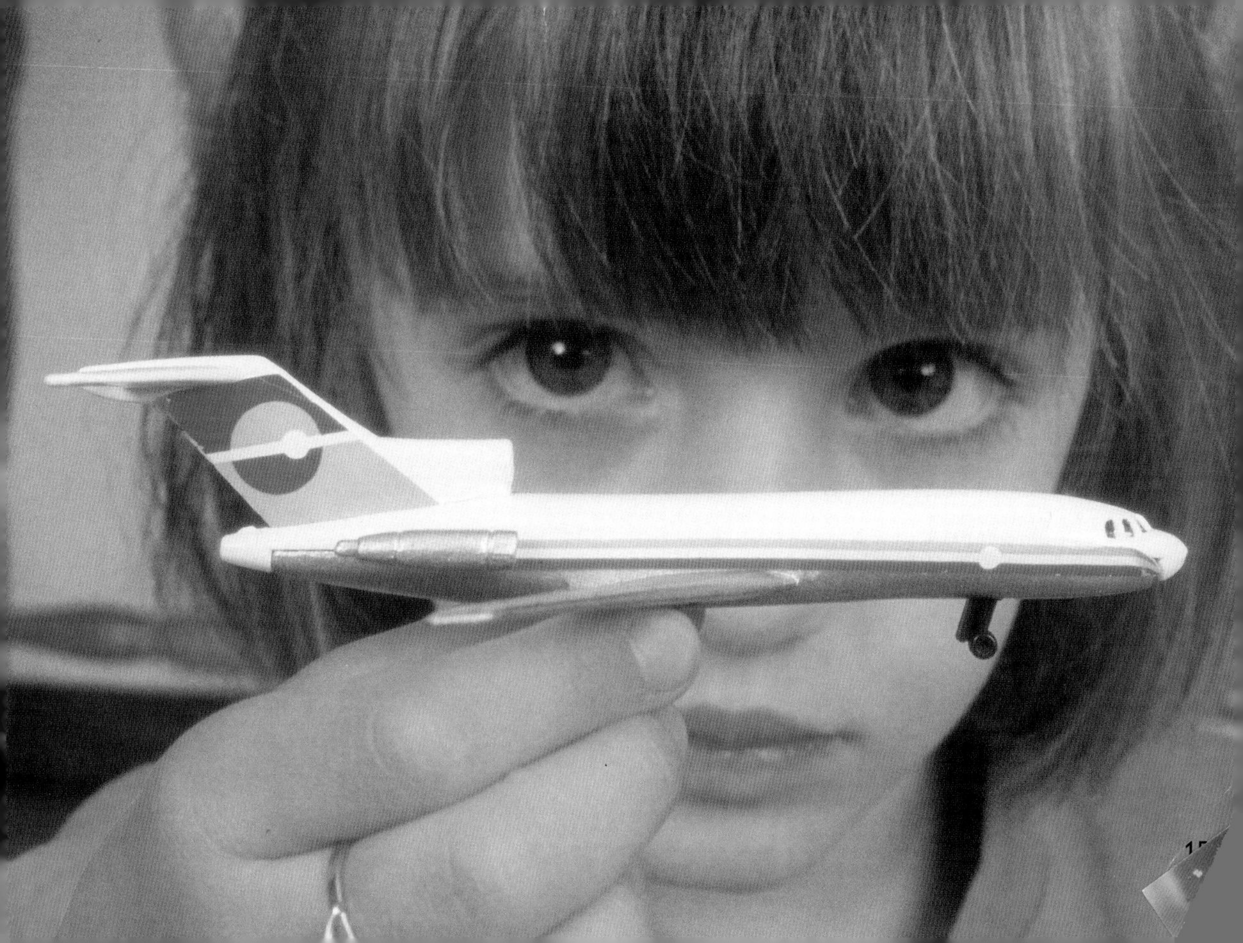

My boat is little.

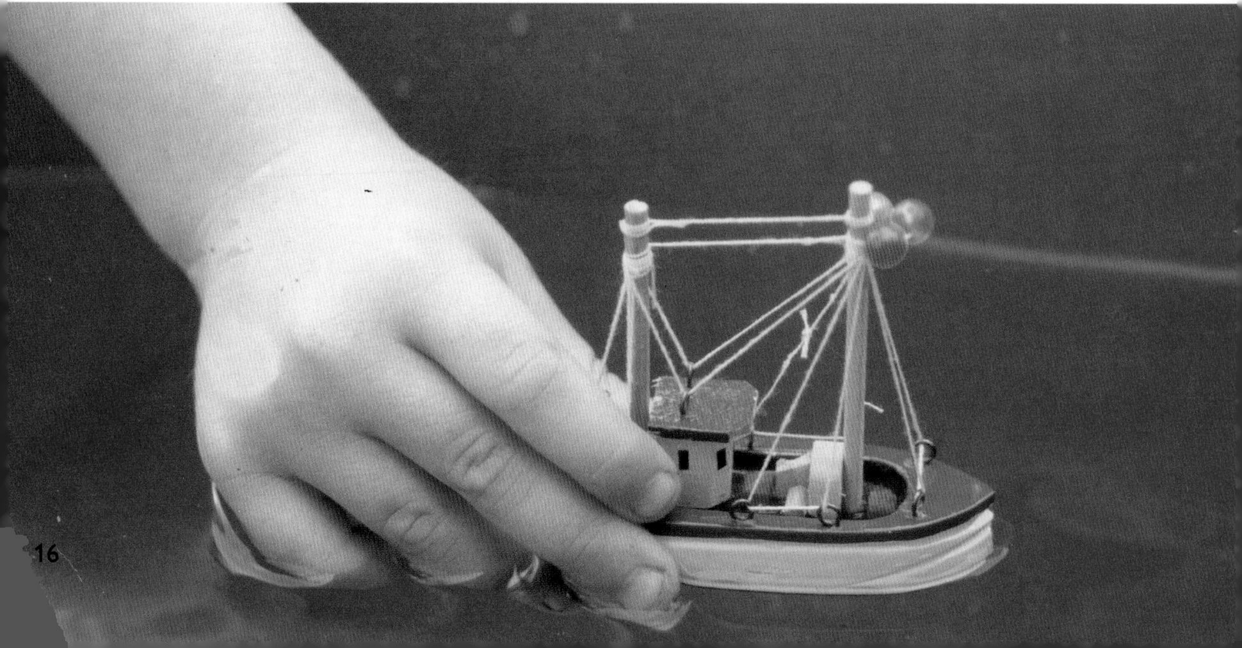